Medicine Bear

Geshiknung (Day Star)

Medicine Bear

Menunqua

C o n t e n t s

v

Introduction

LONG AGO, the Anishinabe (Native Americans) lived in peace and harmony, traveling the Good Red Road of Life. Our Creator, whom we call Grandfather, lowered original man from the sky world to a virtual paradise. He gave him the responsibility of naming all things that had the spark of life of the Creator within them. He also gave him the wolf to help him on his journey.

Original man, whose name was Manahbozho, and Wolf became brothers. They traveled together across the earth, giving names to all of the four-legged, the swimmers, the winged, and the life giving plants that grew from Mother Earth. When their journey ended, Grandfather said to them, "Now you must travel on different paths. You will still be brothers, but Manahbozho must have a mate to replenish the Earth." The Great Spirit then put Manahbozho into a deep sleep, and when he awoke he saw the first woman, Qua (Indian woman).

Manahbozho and Qua learned many things from all of the beings that were named. Each one shared the knowledge that Grandfather had given them. They learned to respect all. And from the sky world, they learned the truths that they would live by.

Now, we the Anishinabe, the original people of this Mother Earth, look back to the time of our Grandfathers. We remember how it was when we lived in peace and harmony with all of creation. As we incorporate the traditional culture and spiritual values of old into our lives today, we become strong again. Our hearts soar when we once more sit around a Sacred Fire and listen to our Elders tell us the ways of our ancestors; the ways that set us free to fly with the Eagles.

The stories that I am about to tell you are truthful accounts of lessons learned by our people since the time of Manahbozho. Sit back and listen carefully for you shall learn the way of the Anishinabe, the way of the Good Red Road of Life.

Young Eagle

YOUNG EAGLE was a boy almost to manhood. He was of the Odawa Nation, Bear Clan, and son of Chief Day Star. His naming ceremony was just yesterday and he was spending his first night in his own lodge. He awoke at dawn, as tired as he was when he lay down on his sleeping furs. It had been late when he finally fell asleep. It was very strange to be alone. He had never been alone before. Oh, sometimes in the forest, when he was snaring Rabbit, he was by himself, but never in the village. He missed his father's lodge. He missed all of his brothers and sisters. He missed his father and mother and his grandfather and grandmother.

This was a very small lodge, made for him by his father and uncles. It was made of maple saplings which had been sharpened on one end and pushed into the earth to form a circle. The tops had been bent toward the center and tied with basswood fiber. Other saplings, lashed together from bottom to top, formed the

1

skeleton of the lodge. Then, birch bark was put into place starting at the bottom and overlapping each row until there was just a small opening at the top to form the smoke hole.

It was cozy and warm inside. Young Eagle had decorated the lodge with the gifts he had received at his naming ceremony. His shield was very colorful with the design that his father had painted on it. His deerskin shirt, breech cloth and leggings, made by his mother, hung from the polished antlers that his brother had given to him for just such a purpose. Beautifully seed-beaded moccasins, medicine bag, knife sheath and sash adorned the lodge also. These were his ceremonial clothes. They would be worn only on important occasions. The porcupine quilled bag for his arrows, made for him by his aunts, showed an eagle perched on the top of a tall pine tree. The bow, a gift from his uncles, stood beside it. He could now walk beside his father and his uncles as a man, instead of following behind as he did when he was a mere boy.

As Young Eagle slipped an arm from the warmth of the furs to put some kindling on the fire, he thought of the lessons that he would learn today. Today was his time in the forest all alone. He would use all that he had learned from the men, when they told of their time of transition from boy to man, around the sacred fire. He excitedly arose to greet the new day.

As he bound his loins and slipped on the worn moccasins, he remembered the many times that his mother and grandmother had warned him about going into the forest alone. "You hear that?" Nokomis would whisper. "You hear Bear? You hear Wolf? They're hungry, those animals. They're big and fierce and will eat you if you go into the forest alone. Stay away from that place until you are a man." His small body would shake with fear at the thought of being eaten by those huge beasts. Grandmother was right. "I'm not going to go near that place," he would say.

2

Apprehension replaced the excitement that Young Eagle had just felt. A tickle of remembered fear ran up his neck at the thought of going into the deep dark woods alone. "But you are almost a man now, Young Eagle," he said aloud. "My sleeping furs are from Bear, the largest animal in the forest. My father killed him with his arrows. My father is not afraid, and so, I will not be afraid." Young Eagle pushed back his fears and stood tall in the bright sunlight outside of his lodge.

As Young Eagle approached the sacred fire, which was just outside of the Chief's lodge, he saw that the men already were seated with their sacred bundles open, lying upon Mother Earth, before them. As the ceremony began, he took his place of honor beside the chief, Day Star. His usual position had been with the other young men.

The circle of men sat upon Mother Earth, waiting for the fire keeper to smudge them with the three sacred medicines. Bunches of sage, sweet grass, and cedar would be set afire from the sacred fire, and then put out with a twist of the wrist. The resulting smoke would envelope and purify each man, as the fire keeper smudged them from their toes to the top of their heads. The ceremony ended when each had smoked from the great Sacred Pipe that Day Star passed around. Tobacco was the fourth sacred medicine.

Now was the time for Young Eagle to enter the forest and travel to the hill, where every Anishinabe boy went to become a man. His father gave him a knife, which had been smoothed and sharpened from a special Grandfather rock called "flint." The knife rested in a plain deerskin sheath. Young Eagle tied it around his waist and was thankful to have such a powerful weapon to take with him into the dark woods. Although he did not look back, he knew that they watched him as he ran swiftly through the trees.

He stopped, when he knew that they could no longer see him, and rested under a giant oak. "Ahwah," he said softly, "my insides growl with hunger." He reached to one side and snipped off the top of a few of the mushrooms that were growing there. He pulled some wild onions and began to eat the delicious gifts of Mother Earth. With his hunger satisfied, he stood and looked around him to get his bearings. It was almost mid-day. He knew that he had to reach the place where the spirits talk, before the day left.

As he ran, his tall well-muscled body served him well. His moccasins barely touched the earth. He made no sound. The long, resplendent, raven hair, trailed behind him as if it were a living thing. His brown skin glistened with perspiration, but his breathing was slow and even and his gait was steady and sure. The blue jay's loud squawking announced Young Eagle's presence and the small ground animals scurried away as he passed. He stopped, lay down to rest, and looked up at the waning light of day. I should have been there by now, he thought. When the men told of their time on the hill, they did not say it was so far.

Bear's deafening roar split the silence of the forest. Wolf's mournful wail rose in protest. Startled, Young Eagle jumped to his feet, and as he ran, stumbling in his haste, the hairs on his forearms stood on end. His old boyhood fears arose and he blindly crashed through the brush. Then the voice of the Great Spirit came to him. "Young Eagle! Would you hide in a tree top or be cornered in some dark cave by your brothers, who have come to teach you?" Young Eagle stopped. He could hear Bear's and Wolf's menacing growls coming closer. How can I go into battle with only this knife, he wondered? but, I can make a strong bow and arrows as I have been taught. He remembered. He remembered his teachings.

Young Eagle raced toward the hill of the spirits. While running, he watched every tree, hoping he would soon find the right one to make his bow. He jumped up and grasped a green branch from a strong young maple. His weight tore it from the tree and he cleaned it and fashioned it into a bow as he ran.

Still running, Young Eagle ripped away part of a basswood tree's bark and took the inner bark and twisted it to form a small flexible rope. He notched the ends of his bow with his knife, tied them so that the fibers were taunt, which then bent it into a semi-circle. He placed the bow on his back, the knife back into its sheath, and with both hands free he watched for the small trees that would be his arrows. When he found them, he raised his head and asked Grandfather for the life of these little ones. Slowing, he bent low, and choosing the straightest, pulled them from Mother Earth. The hard pointed root made a perfect arrow head.

He now ran with protection. He could no longer hear the cries of Bear and Wolf. Smiling to himself, he thought that they must have given up the chase when they realized that he could destroy them! He sat down to rest at the bottom of the hill. He was tired after all of that activity, but soon he arose and climbed to the top. He knelt and raised his face to his Creator. With his arms raised and his palms up, he gave thanks to Grandfather for this day, all his gifts and all of the lessons that he had learned. Young Eagle asked for the life of the maple saplings that he needed. He then engaged himself in constructing his lodge, with the door facing the Eastern direction. He then made a fire pit and gathered some dry wood from nearby to make a fire.

As he sat before the fire that he had kindled with the bow, Young Eagle smoothed the pointed roots and notched the opposite ends of his arrows. He then stood and asked Grandfather for the life of Rabbit. Leaving the fire, he went to hunt. He was uncertain that he could find Rabbit because the shadows were very long. But his fears were unfounded.

He returned to the fire, prepared the meat and placed it onto the cooking rock. He covered it with a green burdock leaf and waited for the meat to brown. Then he lifted the leaf and turned the meat over to brown on the other side. Now, while he waited for his meal to finish cooking, he cleaned and stretched the rabbit skin. When it dried, he would make a bag to carry his Sacred Tobacco.

Young Eagle ate a small piece of the succulent meat and placed the other strips over the fire to dry. He would need to sustain himself during his time here, where the spirits talked. He then fashioned a basket from the birch bark that he had gathered to cover his lodge. This would hold water which he had yet to find. When darkness was upon him, he crawled into his shelter and, lying upon Mother Earth, fell into a deep sleep of peace and harmony.

Young Eagle awoke in the twilight of the morning and went out to the fire to greet the new day. With a green stick, he stirred the flickering embers and placed a piece of wood in the center of the coals. He reached to remove the dried strips of meat that he had placed over the fire the night before, and felt the warmth of the flames as the wood rekindled. As he talked to his Creator, he saw an eagle circling high above him. "Eagle!" he shouted. "You who I am named for. Eagle! My brother! I am happy to see you today!"

The eagle was a messenger from the Creator. He wanted Young Eagle to follow him. Rising, Young Eagle tied his knife, water basket and medicine bag to his side and, with bow and arrows in hand, he followed the eagle. He had to run very fast to keep up with his brother. As he approached a small rise, he could no longer see the eagle. A flowing brook lay in front of him and Sacred Tobacco was growing nearby. Gathering the red leaves, and mixing them with other sacred medicines, Young Eagle filled his medicine bag and then went to quench his thirst. He thanked Grandfather for this gift. After drinking until he could hold no more, he filled the basket with the cold, clear water from the stream. He looked up to see Eagle watching him from a tall white pine. The magnificent bird bid his screeching farewell and flew away. "Thank you brother," was all that Young Eagle could say.

Young Eagle returned to the hill and offered Tobacco, with part of the feast of Rabbit, to the sacred fire. He sat and enjoyed a small piece of the meat and waited for the spirits to come. As the shadows lengthened, he built up his fire and, using his Tobacco, gave thanks to Grandfather and went into his lodge, again falling into a deep sleep.

When morning came, Young Eagle awoke to the rumbling sound of the Thunders, coming from the Western direction. Flashes of lightning lit up the sky and the rain made his lodge sound like a drum with many drummers. And the Big Winds threatened to remove him from the hill. Offering tobacco, morning, noon and evening, he kept the fire going and stayed warm and dry inside of his haven.

When the darkness came, the rains and winds subsided. Young Eagle went to the strong fire and sat in meditation. He heard the howling of many wolves. Then there was screaming. Terrible screaming, punctuating the night with the terror of some being losing its life. Shivers of fear shook Young Eagle. He sprang to his feet and beseeched Grandfather to keep him safe. Settling again before the fire, facing in the Eastern direction, Young Eagle listened as the owl called from the forest below. Bear joined in with his thunderous voice and their voices blended in an erie, unnatural discord. These sounds did not disturb him. Owl was the most spiritual of the winged and Bear was the spiritual protector of the Anishinabe.

Young Eagle sat in silence, clear to his inner-self. He was still positioned toward the Eastern direction, for he had been instructed by the Elders to keep himself facing to the way of the new beginning. Never looking to the other three directions, he heard the sound of a running, grunting bear. Bear was right in back of him, crashing through the brush, traveling from West to North. Young Eagle could feel the hot breath and smell the overpowering, wet dog odor of the bear. Still, he sat unafraid and silent. He fell asleep right there before the fire.

Young Eagle opened his eyes to a brilliant blue sky and the sound of many birds singing to him. Perched in the trees, they were all different colors and so beautiful! "Thank you Grandfather for this beautiful day," Young Eagle said. "Thank you for your creation." He placed his tobacco upon the fire and arose to meet the new day. Now he looked in all directions. Mother Earth was greener than he had ever known before and the Sun was shining bright in the early morning day. He was overwhelmed.

Young Eagle walked to the brook where the Tobacco was gathered. He plunged naked into the pure waters and washed himself. He walked back up the hill and unstrung his bow, tying it, with the arrows, to the inside of the lodge. Though hunger be his in this morning air, he knelt before the fire and placed the remainder of Rabbit into the flame. He also offered Tobacco and gave thanks to the Creator for the many lessons he had learned. He waited until the fire burned out, then covered it with Earth and made it as it was when he first came. He placed Tobacco over the spot and left this spirit place.

As Young Eagle ran, not in fear but in haste to be with his loved ones, Bear watched him from the log that he was tearing apart to find his meal. He made no sound. Wolf looked, from the shadows of the forest, at the young Odawa, but turned and left in another direction. To them, Young Eagle was one with nature. He was their brother.

As Young Eagle approached the village, he could see the

smoke rising from the great cooking fire. A feast was being prepared for his return. His father, mother, brothers and sisters, the Elders and all of the people of the Bear Clan ran with arms upraised to greet and embrace him. He had left a boy and returned a man. His heart was full.

The War Chief

Mᴀɴʏ ᴍᴏᴏɴs came and went. Young Eagle grew restless. He was tired of the routine days. He longed to put to use his shield and lance. He longed to use his great bow in battle. He dreamed of protecting his people by doing some great deed that would command the respect of all. He could hear them clamor, "Young Eagle the brave, Young Eagle the warrior." But there were no battles, only the stories of conflicts long ago that he listened to intently around the fire. Meanwhile, he and his cousins tested their strength and agility during the mock physical contests that they waged. The older men watched and shouted their encouragement. Like the older men, Young Eagle knew he would need the skills that developed from such encounters. Even his resulting bruises were worn like a badge of honor.

One morning, when the village was just starting to stir, a runner arrived. He told of a war chief that was coming to visit them. Excitement grew in Young Eagle, as in all the young men. They leaned closer to hear every word but no more was said. The traveler told only of his long journey and the people he had met on his way. He was of the Ojibway Nation and his family was Loon Clan. He had come from the Northern Direction and had announced the arrival of the war chief to many villages along the way.

Later, while everyone else rested during the heat of the day, Young Eagle waited on the trail of the Northern Direction. Where once he carried only his medicine knife, he now had his shield and lance in hand. He wanted to be the first to greet this noble war chief. He envisioned how the great war chief would look. A giant he would be with a voice like thunder, brandishing magnificent weapons. He would tell Young Eagle all about his heroic deeds. Whose bow, no one but he could draw. Arrows that never missed their marks. Whose speed and strength, none could match. A lance thrown farther than any. He watched the trail for such a one.

Then, when Grandmother Moon began her vigil, an old man approached. The Elder was walking very slowly, but with a spring in his step. Young Eagle ran to meet him. As he grew near, Young Eagle saw that the man was indeed very old. Long white hair graced his frail body like an opened milkweed pod. Corded hands gently grasped a beautifully carved staff and in the crook of his arm, he cradled a full skin-wrapped bundle.

"Greetings Grandfather," Young Eagle said.

"Hello! My name is Many Thunders. I am Odawa and am Eagle Clan." The stranger spoke in a soft way. "What is your name?"

"Young Eagle is my name and I am also Odawa. My clan is Bear."

Young Eagle lifted the heavy pack from Many Thunders' back and carried it for him. The old man's dark eyes twinkled and he smiled broadly at the young man's display of respect. As they walked toward the village, he told Young Eagle stories that made them both chuckle. Unintentionally, the young brave's heart turned away from war-like things, and he was again in peace and harmony with Creation.

When they reached the village, the people of the Bear Clan came to welcome Many Thunders. They each greeted him and shook his hand warmly. Young Eagle's face fell. He had forgotten to welcome Many Thunders in this wondrous way of his people. He was very embarrassed. The old man, seeing Young Eagle's shame, went to him and shook his hand vigorously.

"Hello!" He said. "Hello! Hello!"

It was as though he had read Young Eagle's mind. The young man felt at ease again and joined in the other's animated conversation.

They took Many Thunders to the Great Medicine Lodge. A fire was going inside and fresh cedar boughs were piled high under the sleeping furs. Why was this place of honor given to this old man? Young Eagle pondered. Wasn't this the place prepared for the war chief who was on his way?

Leaving the elder to his rest, the men returned to the center fire and watched with anticipation, as the special evening meal was being prepared. Young Eagle was troubled. "Weren't they going to wait until the War Chief arrived?" He expected some talk of this, but all was silent. He dared not initiate the conversation because he had just become a man. He waited, but the silence prevailed.

Finally, his father arose and went to the Medicine Lodge, scratched on the flap opening, and announced to Many Thunders that the feast was ready. Day Star and Many Thunders came to the fire together. They sat first and then the others all took their places. The women had cooked the feast, but now they sat with their families. The young boys and girls served. They served the elders first, then the men and women, the children, and at last, themselves.

Before they began to eat, Day Star took a small portion of every food to the Sacred Fire inside of the Medicine Lodge, and placed it in the flames. He offered his thanks to the Great Spirit for this repast, and then returned to the celebration. When the last of the deer, rabbit, beaver, corn soup, and fry bread with maple syrup was consumed, everyone rushed to their lodges to don their finest apparel for the special ceremonies and the story telling.

Young Eagle ran excitedly to his dwelling and pulled on his ghost shirt. This was his protection from harm. This he would wear in battle. He grabbed for his lance and shield, and stood proud and tall with these mighty weapons in his powerful hands. He paused for a moment, imagining how imposing he looked, then he went, joined by the other similarly dressed young men, to the Medicine Lodge.

Sitting in the place of honor, on the heart side of Day Star, Many Thunders conducted the sacred ceremonies of the ancestors. His face was stony and disapproving; not at the solemnness of the occasion, but only when he looked in the direction of the young men. Young Eagle was puzzled. What had he done to gain this disapproval? His mind was in a turmoil, trying to fathom such a transgression.

When the ceremonies were ended, and the two chiefs had returned the sacred objects to their bundles, everyone made themselves comfortable. Many Thunders would tell them the reason that he had come. Young Eagle was tired. He did not want to listen to the old man speak of uninteresting things. His eyes kept darting to the doorway, hoping that the War Chief would appear. Then things would be exciting! Tales of wars and great battles! Stories of bravery and honor! Accounts that would confirm his dreams. But then, out of respect, Young Eagle turned his attention to the Elder who began to speak.

Holding the Sacred Pipe in the crook of his left arm, Many Thunders' voice became very soft. Everyone strained to hear. They knew that when an Elder spoke in this manner, an important message would be given.

"Long ago, on this Mother Earth, our people lived in peace and harmony. The Anishinabe were strong and healthy. Everything was provided by the Creator to insure this good life. Then the young men became restless. Jealousy ruled. Each thought himself to be greater than the other. They thought, I will stand alone, the mightiest of them all! They made themselves ghost shirts, painted with symbols of the most powerful animals, to keep them safe in battle. They invented forceful weapons to kill men. Every argument became the impetus to war upon each other. Many Anishinabe, from many Nations, started their Westward journey to Grandfather's lodge (death).

"The mourning wails of the elders, women and children, could be heard all over Mother Earth. The four-legged, the winged, the water beings and the sky world hid from this tremulous sound. The warriors became fearful to face Grandfather. They painted their bodies to hide from Him. Their hearts became stone. They no longer listened to the Elders. They had forgotten the way of peace and harmony. Their boasting became louder than the crying for the dead. They feared no man. They were mighty warriors.

"Then the eagle came to them and flew to the Western direction. They knew that they had to follow the messenger, for he came only when important knowledge was to be given. They donned their traveling clothing and took only their weapons with them. Meat would be taken during the journey, because these young men were proficient hunters.

"On their way, they met warriors from many Nations. Every

Clan was represented from these Nations. The Westward trails
were full of men, going to the same place. The place where
Eagle led them. Only their curiosity kept them from fighting
with each other. Their pace was rapid and none fell behind.
The trek ended on the third moon. Eagle was perched at the
top of a coppery colored stone mountain, watching, as they
gathered in the meadow below. He gave his shrill cry and flew
away. His duty was finished.

"Gathering in groups, the men made their fires and roast-
ed the meat they had hunted along the way. The familiar
bickering began and soon the night was filled with angry
shouts and aggression that preceded a battle.

"Suddenly the Earth began to shake and the sky was alive
with the power of the Thunders. Soft as a breeze that moves
in the evergreens on a warm spring evening, a gentle voice
that all could hear whispered above the resounding Thunders.
The sky world became serene, as if in deference to a greater
power.

"'Why do you fight and kill each other? Have I not given
you all that you need to live in peace?'

"Slowly the warrior's stone hearts melted. They could hear
the weeping of their people. Digging a great hole into Mother
Earth, they buried their weapons of war. The clear waters of
the river became defiled as they washed the paint from their
bodies. They sat at the fires in remorse, again calling each
other Brother.

"As their tears fell, the voice of the Great Spirit once again
spoke to them. 'I now give you a gift that will end all wars
and help you travel the Good Red Road of Peace and
Harmony.' The Great Sacred Pipe was lowered down."

Many Thunders looked over the fire and into the eyes of
the young men and said, "I was one of those warriors."

Silence overcame Young Eagle and the other young braves.
They retreated from the Medicine Lodge, ripping off their war

shirts. Young Eagle walked west to a clearing and began to dig a pit with his hands and a flat stone. The others joined him. Soon their shirts and weapons were buried and they ran to the stream to wash the paint from their bodies. Then they returned to the lodge where the old man sat talking with their fathers. With their heads lowered, they smudged themselves and went to their lodges to think about this night.

In the dim light of early morning, Young Eagle went to his father's fire. He sat down and looked around for Many Thunders. He asked his father where the old man was.

"He is again on the path to another village."

"Who was he?"

With a twinkle in his eye, Day Star replied. "Didn't you know? He was the War Chief we were expecting."

Little Otter

LEANING AGAINST the outside of his lodge, Little Otter watched the other young men prepare for the hunt. He felt so alone.

"Can I go with you?" he asked in an apologetic voice.

"No," Young Eagle shouted. "No, Little Otter, you would scare away Wahwashgesh, the deer!"

They all began to laugh and poke one another with their elbows. Young Eagle crouched and walked in a side-to-side lumbering gate, imitating Little Otter.

He turned away in embarrassment. He knew he walked that way. In the waters, he'd seen the man who looked like the giant oak: tall, broad and massive. Stronger than all, but ugly! So ugly that the young women turned away, startled at the sight of him.

Though Little Otter felt the impending tears, he couldn't let them see him cry like a woman. So he ran towards the woods, his heavy strides sending pebbles flying in the air. A voice inside of him said, "Little Otter, the Elders and the little ones don't make fun of you. They love you. You treat them with kindness and respect."

"Yes," he whispered back, "I should be grateful." But his thoughts were of the present. The hurt of being rejected, the scorn of his peers, left an empty place within him. As much as he understood why the others didn't include him in their circle, he still longed for their companionship.

He could see the trees now; they seemed to beckon him with their branches, waiting to enfold him in the safety of their embrace. And all around the trees, the winged and the four-legged called an invitation.

"Little Otter, come and we will comfort you."

When he had run far enough into the forest so that he could no longer see the village, he stopped and leaned against a full grown birch. Then he slid down its trunk and with his huge arms drawing his knees to his chest, he began to pray.

"Grandfather, Great Spirit, make me be like Young Eagle! Take this slow, awkward body and give me his swiftness, agility and handsomeness. Let me be quick of mind and respected by all. Like Young Eagle, Grandfather, like Young Eagle."

Oh, he thought, if only he was as swift and agile as the brother that he was named for. Nokomis (Grandmother) had told him many times about how she found him at the edge of the river playing with the otters. Gathering medicine, she heard the giggles of a baby and came upon a "wondrous sight." There he was, sliding in the mud with two Otters. She said that his little round face was so dirty that his fearful tears made streaks down his cheeks. He had tried to run from her, but because of his young age, he could barely walk. So she scooped him up and returned to her lodge, hugging him tightly all of the way. Nokomis never did learn why he was there at the river. Many searched for his parents, but no one had lost a baby, so maybe his mother abandoned him because he was so ugly. But Nokomis, he knew, loved him.

His tears spent, Little Otter listened to the bird's song. Then he heard a rustle beside him and raised his head to see Jid'-ah-moo, the squirrel, pawing through the brightly colored leaves for an acorn. He immediately felt better. His little brother had come to cheer him. Looking up at the brilliant colors, Little Otter knew the peace of this familiar refuge. He had learned much from all of his friends. They accepted him as a part of their world.

"Here 1 will make my weapon for the hunt," he gruffly announced. "1 will make such a powerful weapon that the others will insist that 1 join them to take meat for our people!"

Little Otter's animal and bird companions quieted, as if they understood. They watched as he made three arrows. They watched as he notched the arrows and placed fallen feathers in the groove, then secured the feathers into place with the glue made from fish. They watched as he honed the pieces of flint into a sharp weapon. And finally, they watch as he sewed soft hide together to form a bag to hold his arrows. Though Little Otter constructed a weapon of death, they were not afraid. They knew him well. He would not use this fearsome thing on them. He was their brother and they trusted him.

From then on, Little Otter practiced shooting targets like a knot on a tree or a leaf blowing in the wind. But he never used his flint arrows. Instead, he pulled the straight, sharp rooted, little trees from Mother Earth and used them as practice arrows. He only used his flint arrows to hunt with, and he always hunted alone. And he practiced so much that his bow and arrows became part of his arms. He now shot out of instinct. He never missed. In a split second his eyes saw and his arrow found its mark. He no longer had to think about what he was doing.

One hot summer day, when Little Otter was gathering medicine in the woods, he heard shouts and screams coming from the village. He ran to the top of the hill and saw all of the women gathered in the clearing, yelling and clapping their hands, as if to scare something away. Little Otter ran to the village as fast as his huge body would let him, knowing that all of the other men were out hunting. As he approached them, one of the women shouted,

"Little Otter, come help us! A giant Mukwa came out of the tall grass and tried to take a little one. See his tracks!"

Little Otter bent down and looked. Strong scent rose up from the three paw prints. He smelled desperation and fear. He felt the pain of Mukwa. He turned to follow the track. No blood, he thought. Maybe the great bear wasn't wounded. But what about the prints? There were only three. Only wounded Mukwa attack man.

Later, at the rise of a hill, Little Otter watched Mukwa as he lay trembling at the base of a large sugar maple. His front right paw was dangling, held only by a small piece of skin, and the separated shoulder was evident. Little Otter knew that this bear had been in a death battle with another of his kind. The battle must have been at least a moon ago, because the paw was withered and dry.

As Little Otter listened to the mournful cries coming from the giant beast, he knew that it had been a long time since Mukwa had eaten. He also knew that the bear had been ostracized from his family because he was now different. Little Otter understood his brother. He compared Mukwa to himself and how he felt being a loner. Tears welled up in his eyes as the compassion grew. He knew that he could not destroy such a magnificent life.

Then in an instant, the quiet was shattered by the blood

curdling cry of the giant bear as he rose to his full height, fiercely sounding his attack. The hunters, Man of Dreams, Young Eagle and Day Star appeared a few feet from him, but by then it was too late. They had been following the Mukwa's scent in tall grass. When the grass gave way to moss, they stood up and saw him. They didn't even have time to raise their bows.

But Little Otter raised his bow and his three arrows found their mark within a fraction of a second of each other. The first severed the bear's spinal cord and felled him. The second and third smashed his ribs and now blood spewed from the still beating heart. Little Otter arrived there almost as fast as his arrows. He knelt by the dying animal and wept.

"My brother," he said, "I am sorry that I had to take your life."

As a moan escaped from the giant bear's lips, Little Otter turned and looked into the dying eyes. They knew each other, they understood each other, and for an instant their spirit's were one.

Finally, Day Star and Man of Dreams helped Little Otter to his feet. At the same time Young Eagle showed his exuberance by jumping up and down.

"Little Otter! Little Otter!" he shouted. "I'll skin the Mukwa for you. It is such a huge bear that you killed! That Mukwa would have slain us for sure. But for you, I would now be on my way West to Grandfather's lodge. Little Otter, I am proud to call you my brother."

On the way to the village, Man of Dreams said, "Little Otter, I saw you and Mukwa as one in spirit. You rose from the place where death occurred and traveled with him out of sight into the sky world. A great thundering voice spoke to me from the place where you disappeared and said, 'Medicine Bear.' This is to become your name. The name that the

Creator recognizes you by. Come to the lodge that purifies, and we will make you ready for the ceremonies."

That night Little Otter came from the sacred fire as Medicine Bear. Medicine Bear was a powerful name, he thought. Yes, a very powerful name.

MEDICINE BEAR and Young Eagle became best friends. They did everything together. Young Eagle was confident and demonstrative. All of the young people looked to him for leadership. To Medicine Bear, his friend was his idol. Young Eagle could do anything! His ability to make people laugh was his most endearing quality. Everyone gathered around him when he was about to tell one of his "stories." He made animals talk and do things that human beings did. Medicine Bear thought about one of Young Eagle's stories that made him chuckle with mirth every time he thought of it.

Bear (Young Eagle had said) was looking around for a place to relieve himself. He came upon a giant log that was laying on the forest floor.

"This is a good spot," he said. He sat down with his behind hanging over the back of the log. Pretty soon, Rabbit came hopping along. He stopped in front of Bear.

"Oh Mr. Bear," he said, "you've found a perfect place! Do you mind if I join you?"

Bear shrugged his shoulders. "I don't care."

So Rabbit jumped up on the log and took his position.

After awhile, Bear spoke again. "Rabbit, does me-ze stick to your fur?"

"Why of course not!" said Rabbit.

Then Bear picked Rabbit up and wiped himself.

At the end of that story, Medicine Bear's laughter had sounded all through the village. He couldn't stop. The very thought of what Bear did to Rabbit was so outrageous, that he would start another round of laughter. Pretty soon everyone was laughing. Medicine Bear's laugh was thoroughly contagious.

Making people laugh. That was how Medicine Bear neutralized the hurting inside him when others made fun of how he looked or of how clumsy he was. For example, from the time of childhood, he had suffered from inordinate amounts of gas. But instead of suppressing it, he would make as big a sound as possible, and that would make people laugh. So when the villagers who gathered around him asked what he was laughing about, Medicine Bear made a thunderously hollow sound. Then looking ever so innocent, he pointed to Young Eagle.

Horse People

(Bezhgogshenh Anishinabek)

MEDICINE BEAR was sitting with Young Eagle under a tree at the edge of the village, both whittling on the new flutes they were making. They had reached the age of manhood, and it was time to choose a wife. Young Eagle seemed confident that he could pick any young girl, and she would fall into his arms, but Medicine Bear experienced some of that old doubt about himself. How could any Qua want to be his wife? His thoughts traveled in a whole scenario through a life of rejection and loneliness, without a wife or children. The way he looked did matter, he concluded. Even though the girls were comfortable with him, they never looked at him the way they looked at Young Eagle and the other young men. They never teased him. Young Eagle had told him that teasing was the way a Qua showed that she liked you. No, there had been no teasing.

27

"How are you coming there brother?" Young Eagle asked. "You know that we might have to go a long way to find the village of another Dodem (clan)."

"What?" Medicine Bear's thoughts were interrupted. "Why do we have to go now? Why can't we wait until Mother Earth blossoms again? It will be warmer then, and we will find more food on our journey."

Young Eagle's face beamed as he answered. "Well, I've been waiting to tell you about the place we are going. This place is in the Western direction. It is warm there now! We can start out when the sun rises, and only be cold for a few moons, then the rest of the way will be as warm as it is here when the new green comes to greet us."

Medicine Bear had to give in to Young Eagle. He protested no more. After all, he thought, Young Eagle wanted to go find himself a wife, so who was he to impede this exciting journey. They would have so much fun. He began to look forward to the adventure ahead. As they walked to their lodges to prepare to leave, Young Eagle began to speak.

"You know where we are going? We're going to the place of the Horse People. The elders have been telling us about the horse people for a long time."

"The Horse People?" Medicine Bear was astounded. "Why, that will take many, many moons!"

"Who cares. We're young and free of obligations. I want to find a wife from far away. Someone who is different. Someone who will bring new and exciting things to our village."

Medicine Bear slept fitfully that night. His dreams were of imagined animals he perceived as the Bezhgogshenh (horse) that he had heard so much about.

He woke to a grey, windy day. He could hear the Animoosh (dogs) barking at some early rising animal, and their yips as they made contact with the prey. Probably a Zhgaag (skunk), he thought, but he couldn't smell anything. He shook the sleep away as he arose, and remembered what today was. The day that Young Eagle and he were to start their journey to see the horse people. He lifted the flap and looked outside. The sky was churning with dark clouds and the wind whipped sheets of snow across the village. Many were at the fire already. They were wrapped in their robes of fur to ward off the bitter cold. Medicine Bear was glad that he had the giant bear skin to keep him warm. He stirred his fire and noticed that the ashes were cold. Good, he thought as he dressed in his skins and placed Mukwa's head over his own. The hide was too large to wear loose, so he had tied the hind feet up under to form a pouch to carry necessities for the journey. The front feet were over his shoulders and bound at his waist with the woven leather that was his sash. The load was light for Medicine Bear, even though the Mukwa was very heavy. He left his lodge and started for the fire.

Young Eagle met him half way, and though the day was harsh, they greeted each other with excitement in anticipation of their imminent adventure. Young Eagle's father, Day Star, made room for them, and motioned for them to sit. Nokomis served them Wabose (rabbit) stew and fry bread immediately. She patted Medicine Bear on his cheek and whispered to him.

"Little Otter, make your trip a short one. I will miss you."

She put a pouch of dried meat into his hand, and then went to her own meal. Medicine Bear smiled. Nokomis was still not used to his new name. She preferred the name that she gave him when she found him with the otters.

He ate his fill, then bade his farewell to the elders. Both young men were a little sad to leave them. They talked about their feelings, as they started down the trail that leads to the Western direction. After all, this was the first time that they had traveled all by themselves.

Young Eagle and Medicine Bear ran most of the day. The snow had ended, and the air felt almost warm when they stopped in a valley to make camp. Gahk (porcupine) had crossed their trail a way back, but they didn't take the slow moving animal's life for their evening meal. The elders always told stories about Gahk saving many an Anishinabe's life with its meat. They said that if you are lost and hungry, the porcupine will give his life for you. "So, save this animal until the need arises."

They gathered dry limbs for their fire and soon had it going strong. Then they put some tobacco from their medicine bags into the flames and thanked Grandfather for this place where they would sleep. After Medicine Bear had put down his bundle, he picked up his bow and arrows and went into the woods to look for food. He returned shortly with a very large Amik (beaver), and he proceeded to skin the beautiful animal.

"This brother's hide will make a good gift to give to the Horse People, he said. "I will prepare it while you roast our meat, Young Eagle."

Young Eagle grinned and said, "Ahow! (I agree) The Qua that you chose will wear that over her shoulders with pride, Medicine Bear. She'll just jump into your arms in gratitude! Ha! Ha! Ha!"

They teased each other with boyhood abandonment, and wrestled around until they were exhausted. When their bellies were full, Young Eagle placed the remainder of the meat to dry on the hot stones that surrounded the fire. They would have plenty to keep the hunger away for many a day. Then they fell into a deep sleep.

The trek was long and hard. When the third moon came, they had shed all of their warm clothing and carried it in bundles that were strapped to their backs. They ate of the green things that Mother Earth had provided with her rebirth, and grew strong and lean. Even though Medicine Bear was a foot taller, and much bigger than Young Eagle, he too was in exceptional form. Much more agile, he ran with the ease of Wahwashgesh (deer) and the strength of Mukwa.

The scenery around them began to change. They were now running in tall grasses on open plains. They followed the animal trails, and kept heading in the Western Direction. They had crossed a mighty river, and were glad to be on unimpeded paths. For a while they had traveled in the Southern Direction, but now the sun set ahead of them. They could hardly contain their excitement at the knowledge that their goal would soon become reality. Any time now they would reach their destination, and finally meet the Horse People.

The shaking of the Earth awoke Medicine Bear. There was a loud rumbling sound. "Ahwah!" Young Eagle cried at his side. "The Thunders are great here!"

They looked to the sky and saw many stars. They were totally bewildered. The deafening sound grew closer and closer, and pretty soon a tremendous cloud of smoke rose from the ground to their north. They ran to a small hill to see where the smoke was coming from, and they were amazed to see thousands of animals rushing towards them.

"It's the Horses!" Medicine Bear shouted as he jumped to grab the limb of a scraggly tree. "Climb up here Young Eagle, or they'll trample you to death!"

But Young Eagle stood transfixed as the thundering herd swept past him. Medicine Bear fell from the tree, as the branch that he was standing on broke. The young men talked way into the night about what they had seen. Finally, they fell asleep just as the light began.

The next day, they went to examine the trail of the Bezhgogshenh. The ground was broken as far as they could see. A figure came over the horizon. Another and another came. Soon they could count six men running toward them.

As the men approached, Medicine Bear could see that they were not running. They were riding on the backs of big, long legged animals. The animals and men seemed as one. They slowed down as they approached Young Eagle and Medicine Bear, and shouted greetings. A tall young man jumped off his animal and with a broad grin, grasped Medicine Bear's upper arms.

"Medicine Bear, we have been waiting for you. My name is Wagoshenhs (small fox). I am Cheyenne, and Eagle is my clan. Welcome to this land that we call home. Come, and we will go to our camp where a feast is being prepared for you."

Medicine Bear looked at Young Eagle. How do they know my name? he wondered. They act like they were expecting us, and these animals must be the horses that we have heard so much about. Yes, these must be the horse people, but what were those huge animals that we saw last night?

The mystery was solved as they all walked to the camp. Small fox explained to them that the animals were Puhgocheh' (Buffalo). He said that they had been given by the Creator so that his people could survive in this land of grasses. Now it was time for the Nation to begin their journey to the mountains in the Northern Direction where they would gather medicine and stay for the summer. They had delayed their annual exodus because of the expected arrival of Medicine Bear.

They didn't walk for very long until they arrived at a large village, where everyone was busy packing their belongings onto horses. When they saw the visitors, they rushed to greet Medicine Bear.

"Medicine Bear!" they clamored. "We are honored that you come to us. Sit in this place of honor. Eat of the we-ahss (meat) that we serve you."

Medicine Bear and Young Eagle were still confounded that these people were expecting them to come. There was no one sent before them to announce their arrival. Besides, only very important people were proclaimed by runners, and how could a runner get here before them?

Sitting at the heart side of the Ogema (Chief), Medicine Bear finished his meal, then sat back to reflect upon these mysteries. The Ogema turned to him, smiled, and spoke in the slow, careful way that revealed his authority.

"The War Chief, Many Thunders, has told us about you. He told us how you killed the Giant Bear to save your people. He told us of Man of Dreams' vision that Mukwa's spirit and your spirit became as one, and that you now hold, deep within you, the spiritual medicine of that Great One. Many Thunders said that you will reveal to all inhabitants of this Turtle Island (world), The Great Law of Peace."

Young Eagle looked at Medicine Bear with astonishment. He saw his friend as if for the first time. These people thought that Medicine Bear was a prophet or something! "Wait a minute," he wanted to say, "I'm the one that you should be talking to. I'm the son of the great chief, Day Star. I'm the leader here. He's only the follower. You should have seen him before I befriended him! He was a sorry sight to behold. Nobody liked him. Nobody wanted him around. Sure he killed a bear, but if I would have had the chance, I could have killed that bear too!"

Certain that the others had read his thoughts, the young man hung his head in shame, and remembered why Medicine Bear had taken the Great Bear's life: "Medicine Bear had slain the bear only to save us...Day Star, Man of Dreams and me. So I should be happy that I'm alive. I should be proud of Medicine Bear. After all, he is my brother now, and we have become best friends."

Young Eagle jumped as Medicine Bear forcefully nudged him. He saw that everyone was leaving. Small Fox was gesturing for him to follow. He stood and let them lead the way to the entrance of a cone shaped, buffalo skin covered, lodge. I missed all the talk, he mused, as he bent down to enter. And he couldn't ask what was said because they'd know that he wasn't listening. The exhausted young man snuggled into his sleeping furs and immediately went to sleep.

Young Eagle's dream lasted from the time he closed his eyes until the moment he awoke. He sat at a fire in his father's lodge. All the elders were gathered there with him. They each spoke in turn, and again told Young Eagle the stories that he had heard throughout his life. He was reminded of pure thought, kindness, respect for others and himself. He experienced great remorse for the jealousy that he had displayed against Medicine Bear, and was more than happy to awake and have the opportunity to rectify the transgressions.

The village was already alive with activity when Young Eagle and Medicine Bear stepped outside. They rushed to the river and washed themselves so that they could help with the preparations for the trip to the mountains. When they returned, Small Fox and his comrades were dismantling the lodge that they had been sleeping in. The two Odawa accepted the dried buffalo strips, and they ate their morning meal as they helped with the work. Soon all of the skins were rolled and tied to the horses. The elders and children sat on taut skins that were attached to poles, which were also secured to the horses. Everyone else rode their own Bezhgogshenh except Young Eagle and Medicine Bear. They watched as they walked, and by the time the mountains came into view, they both were sure that they too could ride the horses.

They arrived just before sunset, and everyone was anxious to ready their summer village. It didn't take long until the lodges were up and fires were burning brightly. There were many Cheyenne camps surrounding them. The other clans had been there for a few days, and were already settled. Greetings and laughter permeated the night, and everyone

from the Eagle Clan was invited to a community feast.
Medicine Bear's eyes widened at the sight of so many
Anishinabe. He had never seen so many people!

Then, Small Fox gestured to a very large lodge, which
stood tall in the center of the circle of lodges. It was tightly
covered with light colored deer skin, and was painted with the
many symbols of Creation. The colors, brilliant and true,
reminded Medicine Bear of a crisp autumn eve, of a warm
fire, of the easy familiar time that families spend together
within the safety of their lodge. He was entranced with the
way that the sanctuary glowed and flickered, as if the very
skins were alive. The painted animals and birds seemed to
dance with the beat of the drum, the sound of the heartbeat
of Mother Earth, that was coming from the interior of the
abode. Then, as if he were entering a sacred place, Small Fox
spoke with a soft voice.

"This is the Great Chief's tipi. This is the lodge of
Mishoomis (my grandfather), who is called, Zhingwak (pine).
We will go now, and greet my family."

Medicine Bear and Young Eagle followed Small Fox as he
approached the flap which covered the opening of the tipi.
Small Fox scratched on the flap, and it was immediately opened
by one of the cousins. Enthusiastic greetings were exchanged,
then they were invited to sit at the fire. Starting from the
Western Direction, Zhingwak passed the eagle feather from his
heart side, around the circle, and as each one received the feather, they introduced themselves to the two visitors.

Medicine Bear did not hear any of the introductions. He
did not hear anything but the beating of his heart, in rhythm
with ethereal music from the Sky World. He felt as if warm
water was rushing through his body making him as weak as
a newborn fawn, and at the same time, his whole being tin-
gled, sparked, ignited, as if he had been touched by the fire
that comes from the power of the Thunders.

He watched her, across from him, as she took the feather. She smoothed the fluff with her lissome fingers and slowly raised her head. The long raven hair reflected the fire, and the eyes of a doe met his. Her voice was soft and low.

"Ahnee, Wahwaskwane ndizhnihcauz (Hello, my name is Flower). Gebizhian megwetch (Thank you for coming to visit)."

Wawaskwane

(Flower)

WHEN FLOWER looked into the eyes of the young stranger, her heart jumped in her breast. She heard herself whisper the greetings, but it was as if she were there across the fire with him, touching him, saying her name only to him. They were alone, warm and safe, as if they were one. She felt the strength of his magnificent body as she lightly traced her fingertips across his wide neck, down his shoulders and upper arms, then meeting at the center of his chest. She could feel the strong, rapid beating of his heart, together with her own. Unshed tears tightened her throat, and simultaneously, joy welled up in her until she thought she would burst!

"Wawaskwane." Zhingwak's voice brought her back to the fire. "Wawaskwane, if you are finished, pass the talking feather to your brother."

Flower placed the feather into Small Fox's heart hand and lowered her head. I hope that Young Eagle did not see my spirit, she thought. He would never ask to court such a bold Qua.

She studied the pattern of her moccasins, noting the bright yellow petals of a daisy that the many seed beads portrayed. She counted them, then counted them again, but she still felt as though she were in Young Eagle's arms. As the warmth continued to spread through her, Flower saw their wedding day—daisies in her hair, the white buckskin of a new wife, Young Eagle tall and handsome in his ceremonial skins, and her grandfather, Zhingwak, joining their hands. She felt her first born stir in her, and saw him grow to look just like Young Eagle. She saw many children born of them. Wawaskwane and Young Eagle, husband and wife, growing old together, then going hand in hand into the spirit world.

The drums sounded outside of the tipi. The singers sang of the celebration of life. The dancing had begun, and everyone went to place their footprints on the sacred circle of Mother Earth. Flower arose and went to join the others. She longed to dance alongside Young Eagle, but waited until the young women took their place at the Eastern Doorway. Now they would be ready to follow the men into the circle for Grand Entry.

Zhingwak stood alone at the East entrance to the circle. He carried the staff of the Cheyenne Eagle Clan. It was carved from the tip to the base, and was as long as the old chief was tall. The carvings were of medicine plants, flowers and vines, and at the top was the head of a bald eagle. Wawaskwane knew that the eagle was carved from wood, but it was so real that she was sure that it moved, ever so slightly. As Zhingwak raised the staff, the eagle looked back at her and invited her to join it in the circle. "Come daughter," it said. "Come and dance. Come and dance with me."

The drums sounded low and strong, the vibrations echoing from Mother Earth into the dancer's feet. The singers with their high voices sang of their appreciation for the many gifts that the Great Spirit had given the Anishinabe. They sang about the first man who entered the circle, many seasons ago. The drums called to the men, and they answered with their movements which imitated animals and birds. Then the Grandmothers entered, followed by the younger women, a continuous line of Anishinabe Qua whose feet just brushed the top of the trampled grass as they double stepped in rhythm with the drum. Their movements were slow and graceful, not unlike the butterfly who rides the summer breezes on the way to the delicate rose. The dancers told their stories without uttering a word.

Wawaskwane danced in joyous abandonment. She felt the warmth of the night on her flushed face, and as the breeze cooled her, she watched Young Eagle dance, imagining his lips brushing hers—but Medicine Bear was ahead of her, blocking her view. She noticed that the huge man was almost totally covered with that bear that he always carried. I can't go near him, she thought. He scares me! I'll just dance near the drums on the inside of the circle and maybe I won't have to look. But she still watched him. The giant bear covered all of him except for his face and the front of his arms and legs, and it took a lot of scrutiny to find the man. His dance was very powerful. Everyone's eyes were on him. Flower felt fear of the bear, but a strange attraction to the man.

The drums ended their song and the dancers went to sit at the edge of the circle. Flower went to sit with her Grandmother.

"Grandmother, I need to talk to you. Do you have time for me?"

The old woman smiled and nodded. She pointed with her lips to the tipi that was standing almost out of sight, way up in the woods. Flower knew that it was for the women on their moon time. She wondered how Grandmother knew that her moon time had begun when she was dancing in the Sacred Circle. The two women left the festivities for the quietness of the small lodge. Flower looked around and immediately felt comfortable in the familiar surroundings. Although she had never been in this moon lodge, it looked the same as the one in her winter village. Sleeping places were tucked into the decorated liner, where lush furs covered fresh cedar boughs. They were just an arm's length away from the center fire. She saw two lazy-backs by the lift pole and recognized them as the ones Grandmother had been working on for three suns. The chairs were low to the ground and made of small branches from the wild cherry tree. They were lashed tightly together with basswood fibers, then tied to a heavier frame. Grandmother sat down, reached around in back of her to adjust the chair support to comfort her back, and waited for her granddaughter to speak.

"Grandmother, while I was dancing, my moon time came to me. I am very afraid that in this time of great spiritual power, I have taken power from the men's sacred objects."

"Wawaskwane, you did not enter the sacred circle with such power, and left as soon as you realized your power, so you must not worry that you have caused harm." The old woman pulled a piece of soft deer hide and a horn full of tiny seeds from her bag. The seeds had been dyed many brilliant colors. As she talked she sewed; vines, flowers, animals and birds appeared as if by magic.

Flower was transfixed. I could never sew that fast, she thought. The spirits that care for Grandmother must all be creating the design. She knew better than to interrupt when an elder was speaking, but had a difficult time trying to be silent while she watched Grandmother's gnarled fingers fly.

Without lifting her head, the aged woman spoke again. "I

will now tell you of first woman. First woman's name was Anishinabe Qua. The Great Spirit made Anishinabe Qua to be a partner to first man, Manabozho. she was given the power to cleans herself every moon, if she had not become with child. She was very spiritual, and especially so in her moon time. She had so much power, that if she were near Manabozho's sacred objects, the spirits that dwell within these objects would leave and come to her."

Grandmother looked at Wawaskwane and continued, "Anishinabe Qua's spirits who guided her, told her to go away from Manabozho and build a lodge for herself. The lodge was for her only, when she had so much spiritual power. She was to use this time to rest and do the things that she enjoyed— the things that she usually had no time for. Dreams and visions would be hers. She would see her path in life and the path of the many others after her. She would tell her daughters and granddaughters of these things, and instruct the young men concerning the moon ceremony.

"So, Anishinabe Qua found a place at the edge of the woods near a small running stream. She offered tobacco to the Great Spirit, took small maple saplings and the bark from birch trees, and thanked them for giving their lives for her. Then, constructing her lodge, she sang happy songs—songs that came to her as she worked. She gathered moss from the ancient Mmtig (tree) to hold the unneeded nourishment for a new life, then placed it near her sleeping place. She would give the used moss back to Mother Earth, and Mother Earth would take care of it.

"She neither gathered nor cooked her food. Manabozho would do that for her. He would bring the food near the edge of the woods and place it on the ground. Then when he left, Anishnabe Qua would go and get it and divide it into portions that would fit into the palm of her hand. Each portion would be eaten when her stomach growled."

The old woman shifted her position and went on. "When Gesis (the sun) rose and fell seven times, Anishinabe Qua would leave the moon lodge and wash in the stream. Then she would go to Manabozho, cleansed physically and spiritually, her body preparing anew to nurture a new Binogiin (baby)."

Grandmother carefully placed her sewing into her carrying bag and arose. Wawaskwane, out of respect, stood also. Knowing that her learning time was over, she bade farewell to her elder and stood in the doorway of the lodge watching the old woman make her way slowly down the path as she returned to the festivities. "Binogiin," she softly whispered, as she caressed her stomach. "Binogiin, my babies will rest here."

She watched the dancers as they circled the drum. There was her love, Young Eagle. How beautiful he was, she thought. So strong and graceful, like the panther that roamed these mountains. Warmth ensued her, the same feeling that she had when she first looked into his eyes at her grandfather's fire. Then above her, Megeze's shrill cry pierced the night sky. The drums stopped sounding. The singers stopped singing. The dancers stopped dancing. They looked up to see the silhouette of a great eagle, illuminated by Nibik Geesis (Grandmother moon), circling and calling. He called four times, then disappearing in the Western Direction, he dropped a feather. All was hushed. All was still. All watched as the perfect feather swayed back and forth, slowly falling to Mother Earth.

The feather rested at Young Eagle's feet. Young Eagle and the feather were both encased in a capsule of white shimmering light. The light of Nibik Geesis. The men all gathered around and the drums sounded. Young Eagle reached into his tobacco bag and gave some of the sacred medicine to Zhingwak. Zhingwak put the tobacco on Mother Earth, close to the eagle feather. Wawaskwane knew that he had asked the elder to retrieve the feather for him. She remembered the story that Zhingwak had told her and her cousins when they were children. The story of Megeze. The story of Megeze and the perfect feather.

A LONG time ago, when the Earth was new and the Anishinabek were created, the Great Spirit told the eagle to watch over them for him. He said that if he found one who was true of spirit and who did, or was about to do, a great deed, Megeze was to drop his only perfect feather for this honorable one. The eagle grew only one perfect feather in his lifetime, so he chose the receiver with great certitude.

Because the four legged, swimmers, and winged always obeyed the Creator without question, Megeze watched his perfect feather grow and groomed it carefully. He was so excited! "Who will I drop the feather for?" he thought. "Would it be Manabozho, Anishinabe Qua, or another of their Ododem?" Megeze waited, it seemed like forever until the perfect feather was ready. Then he observed the Anishinabek as Grandfather told him, waiting—waiting.

One day he was sitting atop a tall pine, watching for food. A Wahwashgesh ran from the edge of the woods to right under the same tree. Two men ran after the deer, stopped, then shot their arrows. The deer fell immediately. They started to argue about whose arrow had killed the animal. The argument escalated and they began to fight. One man pulled out his knife and slashed at the other. The other's nose was cut from his face. Then, with blood streaming through the fingers of the one hand that covered his wound, the other hand reached down to his side and pulled out a large skinning knife that was tied there. He stabbed again and again. The one who had disfigured him lay dead.

Megeze watched intently. He had never seen the Anishinabek display such violence! The bearer of the knife stood silently with his head down, showing great shame for what he had done. Megeze followed him as he walked back to his village and sought out the family of the man he had killed. As he called the names of the man's family, the whole village came out from their lodges to see what was happening. The father and brothers of the murdered man, came to No Nose and stood in front of him.

No Nose handed the father the bloody knife and said, "I have killed your son. You must now kill me."

"'I will not kill you," the father spoke as he handed back the knife. "One life cannot be taken for another."

With blood still streaming down his face, No Nose went to each of the brothers with the same result. He then offered the knife to the grandfather and uncles. No one would take revenge. He ran away from the village. He traveled far away from the place that he had always been, and Megeze followed him. When No Nose prayed, the great eagle carried his prayers upon his wings to the Great Spirit. So Megeze knew the sorrow of No Nose. He watched him for many seasons, and when the broken man was the most sorrowful, Megeze dropped his perfect feather at No Nose's feet.

No Nose picked up the feather with awe. He look up at Megeze, still circling above him, and said, "Gebihzhian Megwetch" (Thank you for coming to visit). No Nose knew that the time for sorrow was at an end. He also knew that that perfect feather would protect him for the rest of his life.

The sound of the drums brought Wawaskwane back to the present. She heard the singers begin the honor song: "Way ah ha, way ah ah, way oh hay, way oh hay, way ah ha, way ah ha, way oh hay, oh hay, oh hay. Megeze me no nah, Megeze me no nah, wah be bah, me gwan nah, way ah ah, way ah ha..." (the eagle I dreamed, the eagle I saw....)

The men danced around Young Eagle and the eagle feather. They waved their fans from the feather on the ground, gradually upward to the sky world. Then when Megeze flew out of the light of Grandmother Moon into the darkness, Zhingwak picked up the feather and handed it to Young Eagle. Young Eagle and Zhingwak led the dancers in a joyous celebration dance. After they circled once, all of the dancers joined them. It was a sight to behold! Wawaskwane shivered, then went back into the moon lodge. She put some wood onto the fire and sat next to it to remember the many wondrous events of the day.

Little did she know when the day began, that she would meet the man she wanted for her husband. She had no preparation for the intense feelings that overwhelmed her when he entered her grandfather's lodge. She had watched his every move, and she was painfully aware of similar feelings toward Young Eagle emanating from the other young women who were also gather there. She saw again the way they softened and the way their voices became husky and low as they told him their names. Did his gaze linger a little longer on her? "I think it did," she whispered aloud. "I hope it did."

Then, as she undressed and lay down on the soft cedar boughs, she thought of the other young stranger, Medicine Bear. Why was I so afraid of him? It was as if I was startled by a huge mukwa in the woods. He is so big! And he looks so mean! But he acted so kind and gentle, almost as if he was apologizing for the way he looked. She remembered the way his mournful eyes watched her across the fire. It was the look of a little one who watches its mother hold close to her breast a new baby brother or sister, knowing that he would never know that special closeness and love again. Flower's fear faded, replaced by a mother's fierce instinct to protect her child and to erase that terrible hurt. Love flowed through her. She would make sure that Medicine Bear was treated well while he was here with her people. "No one had better make fun of him or I'll make them sorry they did!" She jumped at her own stern voice and as she pulled the furs up around her shoulders, a little smile carried her into the soft warmth of sleep.

As first light washed away the darkness, Wawaskwane looked up through the smoke hole and saw many small birds perched on the tipi poles, greeting the new day with their happy songs. There was no need for a fire, she thought, because the sun made the inside of the lodge warm and cozy. She sang a little song with the birds and told them that they didn't have to move. There would be no smoke to chase them away.

Flower slipped the soft deerskin dress over her head and smoothed it down her body. It was too tight at the breast and hips. "Awah!" she said as she noticed that the skins would stretch no more. "I will make a new dress while I am here in the moon lodge. There will be plenty of time to make it real special, so special that Young Eagle's eyes will follow me when I pass near him. I will make new moccasins and leggings too, and bead them all with beautiful flowers, because my name is Flower.

She picked up the water carrier and went outside to the river, then walked downstream until she found a place to take her morning bath. The river was narrow here where the beavers had built their barriers, but some water still forcefully spew through the piled timbers to make a fast running brook. Flower took off her dress and stepped carefully over the moss covered rocks until she reached the place of the spraying water. She held in her hand the leaves of the cleaning plant that she had taken from the shore. She jumped as the cold water danced against her skin, then crumpled the leaves and rubbed herself all over the make a thick suds. She looked down into the water and giggled. "I look like a grandmother with all this white hair!"

Then she rinsed herself off and stepped out of the water

onto the soft grass of the shore, took some dry moss from the exposed roots of an ancient tree, and placed it to catch the power that flowed from her. She wrapped a small piece of deerskin around her to hold the moss in place then sat on a fallen log to let the sun dry her. She ran her fingers through the shimmering black hair that hung to her waist, and as it dried, she thought about Young Eagle. She wondered if he would come to her father's lodge and ask to court her. Her father would probably growl at Young Eagle and tell him that his little girl was too young to even think of a husband. It had happened before. Flower thought of how the new men looked at her when her body had changed. One even built up his courage to play her a love song on his flute. Her father had chased him away. Her mother sat talking quietly to him for a long time that night, and he sheepishly avoided her for a few days. Then her mother had talked to her, telling her the stories of young love and the instructions of the elders regarding the responsibilities of Anishinabe Qua.

Wawaskwane spent her time sewing, beading, and learning many lessons from the spirits of the moon lodge. Her grandmother, mother and aunts came to visit with her and bring her food. It was a good time. She was happy to be a woman and share this special time with the women of her family. She left the lodge a different person. The girl that came here six suns ago, no longer existed. She was now Wawaskwane, Anishinabe Qua.

And the Spirits Danced

DURING THE summer moons, Young Eagle and Medicine Bear learned the way of the Cheyenne. They traveled to the valley where the horses gathered and practiced catching and taming them. Of course Young Eagle became very adept in this endeavor and predictably, Medicine Bear had a difficult time even getting close to the animals. The horses lifted their heads and sniffed the air as he approached. Seeing and smelling a giant bear, they turned and flew like the wind to the mountain, leaving only clouds of dust rising from Mother Earth. The young men were overcome with laughter at the sight of Medicine Bear, standing in the midst of them with a bewildered look on his face. Then he recognized the humor of the situation, threw back his head and bellowed out his unmistakable roar. The sound was so infectious that a crowd of people gathered and began to add to the celebration. Even the horses stopped and turned to watch.

No longer could they concentrate on the catching of horses. Everyone asked what had happened to cause such merriment, so a fire was started and Small Fox told the story of Medicine Bear's predicament. Of course he embellished quite a bit and as the story grew, the laughter increased until everyone's eyes teared and their stomach's hurt. The young men all chipped in with their point of view and Medicine Bear enjoyed every moment. They weren't laughing at him, they were laughing with him. He was the center of attention. They liked him. The children crowded in as close as they could and kept touching his clothing, his bear, his huge hands, and one even put her hands on his cheeks and forcefully turned his head toward her so that he would pay attention to what she was saying.

During the festivities, the women had prepared a feast meal and while they were eating, many took turns telling stories about attempts to catch horses. The mood was so gay that the stories were about the humorous events that happened at these times. Laughter was always present, so to show respect for the story teller, some would hold their hands over their mouths so the laughter wouldn't interrupt the interesting tale. Then Zhingwak's son, the war chief Meengun Kadeh (Black Wolf), who was Wawaskwane's father, began to tell of the great white horse who eluded all. The mood immediately changed. They all listened closely, especially Medicine Bear and Young Eagle, for they had seen this spirit horse when they were in the valley.

Meengun Kadeh's voice was hushed. His huge body seemed humbled as he spoke. "The Cheyenne have named him, Noodin, for the wind. Noodin is so fast that no one can even get close to him. All the men have tried to catch him, but to no avail. Noodin's appearance is not of this world. He appears as an apparition, long white main and tail trailing behind him as he runs, and he is totally white. But I have seen him when he was unaware of me. When the moon was high last night, I went for a walk. I sat on the hill and watched Noodin and his mares in the valley. He looked up at me before he sped away, and his eyes were as blue as the sky this day."

Wawaskwane's mother put her arm around her daughter's shoulders and pulled her close. She thought back on the night before when Young Eagle came to their lodge to visit. She knew that he had come to court Wawaskwane. He told the stories of his youth, and she watched as her daughter's love for him lit up her face. Young Eagle exuded the magnificent countenance of a hereditary chief. He was big and handsome and bested by no one. She knew that he had never felt heartbreak, though many had suffered heartbreak because of him. Oh, she saw that he didn't mean to hurt anyone, but she had watched the young women sit close to him, waiting for even a glance their way. They sang songs of love in his direction but it was as if he did not understand these songs. He would smile and glance in Wawaskwane's direction, and Wawaskwane would pretend not to see.

Then, still holding the perfect eagle feather in his heart hand, Young Eagle turned to Flower and said, "I feel the Spring time inside of me. Never has a flower bloomed in the sunshine of my heart until now. The song of the wind is not as loud as mine. I have traveled far. I am the wind. I am yours."

She saw that Meengun Kadeh was stunned. He could not ignore the words of the son of a chief. He looked at Wawaskwane and still saw the little girl who had followed him around, idolizing him, now looking at Young Eagle in the same way. She knew that he felt lonely and old. He left the fire and went to his sleeping furs, signifying that the talking was over and Young Eagle must leave.

Flower's mother now watched her husband as he began to speak, his voice holding the authority of his position. "My daughter is now a woman. She is ready to be a wife. I will no longer chase away the new men who try to court her. But I tell you now that the man who takes Flower as his wife will have to catch the great white spirit horse and bring him to me. I will consider no man worthy of Flower that is not capable of catching and taming Noodin."

The young men gathered together and whispered among themselves. "Well, Wawaskwane will be without a husband for the rest of her life," Young Eagle said. "No one can catch that horse! But I'll try again. Flower is a beautiful Qua. I would like to have her for my wife! Let's try again tomorrow. Maybe if we go to Zhingwak, he will pray for us with his pipe."

The men split into small groups, planning their strategy to conquer Noodin. Medicine Bear said he would help Young Eagle. He knew that Wawaskwane wouldn't even consider him as a suitor, but he would help his friend. They went to the lodge of Small Fox, Flower's brother, and talked well into the night. He made many suggestions to help them because he admired Young Eagle, the son of a chief. He secretly hoped that Young Eagle would catch Noodin and become part of his family.

At first light, Small Fox, Young Eagle and Medicine Bear went to Zhingwak's lodge. They gave him tobacco and asked for prayers to catch the spirit horse. Zhingwak smiled at the three's anticipated success. Oh, the enthusiasm of the young, he thought. For a moment he wished that he were young again and could go on the hunt himself. He relived the day long ago when he took two buffalo and gave the hides to Onzie Qua's (Angel Woman's) father. Onzie Qua had been a good wife to him and gave him many children. They had been happy together. And now, as their journey to the spirit world was drawing near, they enjoyed helping their grandchildren through the difficult young years of their lives.

Young Eagle, Medicine Bear, and Small Fox, left Zhingwak's tipi to go to the hill and watch for Noodin to appear. They had planned to observe the horse and learn his ways. If they could only find out where he ran to when he was chased, they thought, they could be there waiting for him when he was tired. Then it would be easy to catch him. They sat on the hill and watched the valley as they wove basswood fibers into strong ropes. They knotted the center of the ropes into a bridle which would slip over the horse's nose, and fit snugly in back of his ears. The bridle wouldn't be so tight as to hurt the animal. They knew that any creature would be your friend if you loved and respected it. The elders told them many times how to gentle a horse. Animals were made free by the Creator, just as the Anishinabe was free. None was to be forced to do another's will. So they made the ropes strong, not to cause Noodin pain, but to teach him friendship.

Medicine Bear had trouble making his bridle. These big fingers are so clumsy, he thought. Small Fox came over to help him, and as they worked, a large group of mares came into the clearing below and leading them was the great white horse.

"Awah!" Young Eagle whispered. "He's so big! I'll have to have a boost to get on his back when I capture him." They laughed at Young Eagle's attempt at humor. But Young Eagle was serious. He knew that the horse was to be his.

Two groups of young men sped down the hill on their horses, and headed for Noodin. Noodin flew like the wind, out of the valley and toward the mountain. He left them in his dust. But they persisted until their horses were white with froth and out of breath. Medicine Bear, Young Eagle, and Small Fox, watched Noodin as he easily outdistanced his pursuers. They saw where he stopped to rest. They mounted their horses and slowly proceeded in that direction. They taunted the young men who were stopped, caring for their exhausted horses.

"Thanks for tiring him out for us. We'll find him and bring him back here to show you how gentle he really is!"

They rode on, heading for the mountain where Noodin was resting. Young Eagle led them far past Noodin's refuge. He asked Small Fox to stay close by the horse and to chase him toward himself and Medicine Bear. Small Fox stopped in a line of pines and waited, watching Young Eagle speed toward a far off clearing. Medicine Bear, although his horse was running as fast as it could, fell way behind. Small Fox laughed to himself. Well, he thought, that's the only horse that was big enough to hold the great weight of Medicine Bear. He remembered when Young Eagle and Medicine Bear caught their horses. Young Eagle had no problem. He had learned well. He picked the fastest he could find and caught and tamed him right away. But Medicine Bear didn't play by the rules. After their initial skittishness at his huge countenance, he talked gently to the horses and they just loved him. They weren't afraid of him at all. Horses were always following him around, jostling to get the best position close to him. He would pull big bunches of green grass and feed it to them, and they would nuzzle him and talk back to him in the way of horses. One large brown and white mare dominated the group, so naturally Medicine Bear rode her the most. He had tried to ride the others, but he was just too heavy for them. He told them that he didn't want to hurt them, and it seemed like they understood. But, Small Fox thought, they sure seemed disappointed!

When Small Fox looked again, Medicine Bear and Young Eagle were no where in sight. He carefully moved through the pines to look for Noodin. He could hear him moving around in the underbrush. Then he saw the great white horse casually eating the lush grass of his hiding place. Small Fox waited, watching him. Oh, I'd love to have him for my own, he thought. But my father said that only a worthy suitor of my sister, Wawaskwane, would bring the horse to him. And I would rather have Young Eagle for my brother than any other. Small Fox watched the sun and when he thought that Young Eagle and Medicine Bear were far enough away, he yelled and waved his arms while running toward Noodin from the rear. Noodin bolted and sped away. Small Fox jumped on his horse and chased him.

The spirit horse was far ahead of him but as he tired, he almost caught up to him. Small Fox could see Young Eagle and Medicine Bear now, and as Noodin passed them, Young Eagle took up the chase on his fresh horse. Medicine Bear and Small Fox trotted behind, knowing that they couldn't catch Young Eagle anyway. There was no longer the need to be silent, so they excitedly talked about what if Young Eagle caught the horse and how he would tame such a wild one. Medicine Bear happily called out greetings to the animals and birds that they met on the way, and he told Small Fox stories to make him laugh.

Then over a rise, they stopped their horses and in disbelief watched as Young Eagle put his bridle on the frothy, panting spirit horse. He leaped easily upon Noodin's back and grinned at them. Then Noodin got his second wind. The giant horse started jumping straight up and down, swiftly turning at the same time. Young Eagle was taken by surprise. A puzzled look crossed his face as he was thrown forcefully sideways. He slammed into the rocky hill and Medicine Bear heard the sharp crack of bones breaking. Medicine Bear jumped from his horse and rushed to where Young Eagle lay. Tears rolled down his cheeks and a great roar arose from deep inside of him. Young Eagle was crumpled and bloody. His spirit struggled to free itself from the dying body. Medicine Bear sagged to the ground and lifted Young Eagle as if he were a child.

He held him close and pressed his giant head against his brother's face. He sobbed and rocked Young Eagle for a long time as the young warrior died.

Then Small Fox heard drums and singing coming from above them. He looked up and saw seven Anishinabe, dressed in ceremonial clothes, dancing down from the sky world. They were singing the honor song, the Eagle Song.

"Megeze me no nah, wah be bah me gwa nah, Megeze me no nah, way ah ha, way ah ha...."

The mountains reverberated with every beat of the drum, and the singing echoed throughout. The dancers were bathed in brilliant white light, and as they descended, Medicine Bear, still cradling Young Eagle's body, stood up to watch the dancers grow near. Then Young Eagle's spirit rose from his body, dressed in the ceremonial skins that his family had made for him such a long time ago. He started dancing with the others, bathed in the same white light. He danced better than he had ever danced before. He was so joyous, Medicine Bear thought. They watched until the dancers went out of sight into the sky world. And Young Eagle waved and grinned at them as he faded into the blue.

Small Fox stood transfixed, holding the reins of Noodin. He looked over at Medicine Bear who still held Young Eagle. Then Medicine Bear placed his friend's body on the back of Noodin and talked to the horse a long time, telling him to walk gently with his brother. They all silently walked back to the village.

Wawaskwane had been sitting under a tall pine tree all day, beading her new dress. She had been watching for the young men to return from their hunt for the spirit horse. When she saw Medicine Bear leading the great white horse, the spirits shouted to her that Medicine Bear was to be her husband. Then she saw that the horse was carrying something. Was it a deer? Where was Young Eagle? Her brother,

Small Fox, was following. His head was down and his body slumped as if he was drained of his life blood. The whole scene seemed as if in slow motion to her. She jumped up, beads flying everywhere. Her heart knew before her eyes could comprehend the truth. "Young Eagle!" she screamed. "Young Eagle!"

She saw his long black hair brush the ground as the horse came toward her, his hands skimming the tall grass as they swayed to the horse's step. She watched as Medicine Bear lifted Young Eagle from the horse and held him in his arms as if he were a child. Then he brought Young Eagle to her. Her tears washed the blood from his face and her caresses groomed his appearance as if to bring back the life that was gone forever. "Cah, cah, cah." (no, no, no) Her voice was as gentle as a mother who soothes her child's hurt. "I love you. I love you."

Zhingwak saw them coming. The giant Medicine Bear, his brother's body in his arms, and Flower holding the lifeless hand of Young Eagle. The great white horse followed and then Small Fox, who was leading the other two horses. Zhingwak picked up his sacred bundle and stood outside of his tipi, waiting for them to come to the medicine lodge. The sky grew dark and the thunders sounded in the low and rumbling way of an approaching storm. The women gathered and began their high pitched warble. The sound of grief. The sound that women had made from the beginning of time. Meengun Kadeh led the men of the village to meet Medicine Bear, Wawaskwane, and Small Fox. In silence, the group took Young Eagle into the women's lodge and placed him upon Mother Earth. Then the men went to the medicine lodge and took their places around the sacred fire. The pipe carriers opened their bundles and arranged their sacred objects in front of them as they sang honor songs for Young Eagle. Their prayers were the prayers of their grandfathers, given to

Manabozho by the Creator at the beginning of life here on this great sacred Turtle Island.

Wawaskwane, her mother, and Onzie Qua, also sang songs as they prepared the herbs that they had gathered to cleanse Young Eagle's body. They were happy songs of young love and new beginnings. Although they were sad to see Young Eagle leave them, they knew that soon he was to start on his journey in the western direction to Grandfather's lodge, and they didn't want him to linger to comfort them. So they dressed him in his ceremonial clothing and placed gifts close to him to help him on his way. When they were finished, they sat and told the stories of old. The stories of their grandmothers. Wawaskwane told of Young Eagle's life that he had shared with them when he had come to court her in her father's lodge. They all laughed until the tears came because Wawaskwane imitated Young Eagle's voice and mannerisms when he had, in his stories, given the animals human voices.

Then all was silent as the drums sounded. It was time to take Young Eagle to the place where spirits gather. The men placed the body onto a fur-lined berth which had been made with the trunks of young cedar. Medicine Bear laid his giant bear skin over his brother, and together with Small Fox, lifted Young Eagle to his shoulders. They followed Zhingwak up the steep path to where four sturdy poles with a support structure at the very top, had been secured into Mother Earth. They placed Young Eagle's bed upon the platform and tied it firmly, then stepped back to allow Zhingwak to begin the Cheyenne passover ceremony.

"The spirit that went to sleep! Get up! Hear us. The old ones again arise. After you arise, get ready to leave. Do not fear to leave. You will have great help after you arise. Grandfather, Grandmother you will look for. Now you will leave this place. Way up where you will go, not for us to see. At night you will send messages this way. Do not glance back.

Do not glance back. Do not glance back. Do not glance back."

Then, while the drum sounded and the men sang the farewell song, Zhingwak lit his Chi Pwapwagun (Great Sacred Pipe) and offered it up to the four directions, to the center of the four directions, and to Mother Earth.

Medicine Bear thought of the passover ceremonies that he had witnessed back home. He could hear Man of Dreams' voice as he said the same words in the Odawa language as Zhingwak had just said in Cheyenne. As he took his bear skin from the body, so that Young Eagle could see the spirit world, Medicine Bear felt the completeness of his brother's life. Grandfather had called him home. It was his time. He was at the end of his Red Road, beginning a new and exciting life. Medicine Bear smiled as he remembered Young Eagle's grin and wave to him as he danced with the spirits. Then he put on his bear and began to dance. The singers sang the Eagle song, and his big heart broke all over again. Tears streamed down his cheeks. His footsteps made the earth shudder.

The women and children came to join the men. Hundreds and hundreds of Anishinabek now circled Young Eagle, watching as the giant spirit bear bade his last farewell. They all began to sing, "Megezee me no na, wah be bah me gwa nah, Megazee me no nah, way ah hah, way ah hah...." (the eagle I dreamed, the eagle I saw....)

Medicine Bear danced through the night until the sun brightened the new day. Then he went to the river and washed himself clean in the clear, cold water. He rested there in the warm grasses, until the day began to wane. Wawaskwane had watched and when he had begun to stir she brought him food to eat. They sat quietly, peacefully, until darkness overcame them, then Medicine Bear thanked Flower and went to Small Fox's lodge to say his prayers and complete the day.

Neebin Qua

(Summer Woman)

WHEN THE warmth of the days began to fade into cool stillness, the Cheyenne camp began to prepare for the trip down the mountains to their winter home on the plains. Medicine Bear stripped the hides from Zhingwak's tipi, folding them carefully into small bundles so that they would fit neatly on the travois. The horses seemed to know that they were going back to the place where the tall grasses were still green, so they stepped and snorted in anticipation of the fresh, filling feast that awaited them. Noodin stayed close to Medicine Bear, nudging him once in a while, as if to say, "Pay attention to me. I'm lonely." To Medicine Bear, it was almost as if Young Eagle were in back of him saying, "Stop being so clumsy, brother, let me show you how to do that!" Tears blurred the big man's eyes. He blinked rapidly and went on with his labors. Young Eagle was gone, but Medicine Bear still missed him.

After a few hours of concentrated labor, the journey began. Medicine Bear and Wawaskwane had become fast friends. He treated her as a sister, but longed to hold her close and tell her how much he loved her. He dreamed about her day and night, imagining their being together as man and wife, imagining himself as a handsome man, a man worthy of this beautiful Flower. They rode together on Noodin, talking and laughing, enjoying each other's companionship so much that it seemed to them a short time to their destination.

The sun was almost to its resting place when the Cheyenne arrived home. There was a flurry of activity as the tipis were covered and everything was put in its place. Then the children gathered firewood, and the women prepared the evening meal. Everyone excitedly ate and talked about the events that had taken place during the summer in the mountains, and all of the things that they had to do to get ready for winter. The pale quarter moon that they had seen during the day, rose to her full majesty and lit the star filled sky as the village slept. Medicine Bear slept fitfully. His thoughts were of Nokomis. By morning he had decided to start his journey back to the Odawa. He didn't want to leave Wawaskwane, but he felt that he had to go home. The story of Young Eagle must be told. No one even knew that he had been killed.

He arose as the sky began to lighten, wrapped his huge body with the fawn colored breech cloth, which covered his loins, and tied it around his waist with a supple lash of leather. The surplus came up and over the lash to cover his front and back to his knees, but left his legs free. His long thick black hair, which hung to his waist both front and back, made it look like he was wearing a heavily furred vest. He didn't tie it back or braid it because he was going to the river to clean himself for the new day. The moccasins slipped easily onto his feet as he took his tobacco bag and slipped quietly out of Small Fox's lodge so as not to awaken him. Medicine Bear's footprints, twice the size of other mens, crushed the dew covered grass into Mother Earth. I couldn't hide if I wanted to, he thought, my trail is so easy to see.

As he removed his clothing and stepped into the clear, cold, rushing waters, Medicine Bear's thoughts were of Wawaskwane. He saw his beautiful Flower as if she were standing there with him. "Wawaskwane, my love." He spoke in the same deep hushed voice that he always used when talking to her. "How will I ever be able to leave you? My heart will weep for the rest of my life. I will take my love for you into the spirit world, when I make that final journey in that westward direction, to Grandfather's lodge." Big tears rolled down his cheeks as he put his tobacco down at the edge of the river and asked Grandfather for the life of the cleansing plant that he needed to suds himself. He told that plant that he was sorry to take its life, but he must make himself clean for his morning prayers. He crushed the leaves, then covered himself with thick lather from the top of his head to the bottoms of his feet. Wawaskwane's image never faded as his tears made clear paths down his face.

Medicine Bear came through the trees at the edge of the village to find that everyone was sitting at the fire. The smell of cooking meat made a great hunger arise in him. He hurried to sit beside Wawaskwane and take the huge piece of quehzhagun (fried bread) and wawashgesh we-ahs (deer meat) that she held up to him. The sadness that he had felt earlier was replaced with the euphoria that he always felt when he was around the beautiful Flower.

Wawaskwane felt a rush of excitement, a fluttering of her heart, and a surprising flush of heat that encompassed her female being, when she saw Medicine Bear clear the trees. He is so big and strong, she thought. His maleness was over-powering! She hurriedly took the largest piece of meat and put it between the two biggest pieces of bread, then handed it to him as he came to sit beside her. She tried so hard to suppress her feelings, but it was impossible. Each time their arms brushed, or their thighs were close, she could feel the heat build within her. "What is this?" she said to herself. "I didn't even feel this way when I was close to Young Eagle. I loved Young Eagle, but this feeling I have now is different. It is so strong. I want Medicine Bear to hold me forever. I want to feel him inside of me. I want to be his wife!"

Medicine Bear could feel the excitement coming from Wawaskwane. He looked into her eyes and saw the love, the need, smoldering there. He thought he must still be asleep and dreaming! He dreamed this same way of Wawaskwane many a night. He blinked his eyes and looked around. No, he thought, this is real. I can see the fire. I see and hear the people. I taste this food. I feel her love. My impossible dream has come true! Grandfather has heard my prayers! He raised his eyes to the sky world and whispered thank you to his Creator.

After the morning meal, Medicine Bear took Noodin, walked to Meengun Kadeh's lodge, and scratched on the door flap. He was invited to enter so he went to where Flower's father was sitting and gave him tobacco.

Meengun Kadeh, Medicine Bear greeted the Cheyenne chief. "Just outside of your lodge stands Noodin, the great white horse. My brother, Young Eagle, captured this elusive four legged to give you as a gift for your daughter, Wawaskwane, to become his wife. Young Eagle has now left for the spirit world. Now I, Medicine Bear, give you this same gift and tell you that I wish for Wawaskwane to be my wife."

Black Wolf took Medicine Bear's hand and shook it with the firmness that showed his acceptance of the gift of tobac-co, and the horse that flew like the wind. "Mah-dah-bin,

Gah-been-dah-gah-meh!" (Come in and sit, we'll smoke)

As Medicine Bear sat down at the fire, he watched Black Wolf open his bundle, lay out his eagle feathers and pipe in front of him, then slowly fill the pipe with sacred Suma (tobacco). In the same calm deliberate manner, Black Wolf began to speak.

"I, Meengun Kadeh, have watched you and my daughter become close friends. I also observed you as you ate together this morning. I know that you have silently loved Wawaskwane since you arrived many moons ago from the Eastern Direction. Now I see that same love in her eyes. Yes, I will talk to my daughter and my wife then give you your answer." He smiled and went on. "Now, Medicine Bear, tell me of your life."

They talked a long time, then smoked the Sacred Pwa-pwa-gun to show that they agreed upon all that was said. Medicine Bear left the lodge and went to the river to pray. He didn't see Flower for the rest of that day but was still very happy. He knew in his heart that he and Wawaskwane would soon become man and wife.

Winter blasted the plains with powerful winds and dry cutting snow. The long grasses lay plastered to Mother Earth, and the trees were barren of even the meager dried leaves that had clung to the branches just a few days ago. It was a cold dark time for the people of the Cheyenne village. There were very few days of sunshine. The women had gathered well and the men had hunted with much success so there was no hunger, but the storms seemed never ending. When the chores of the day were finished, the people gathered in the lodges to listen to the storytellers spin their magic. They told the stories of old, the history of the tribe, in such a way as to mesmerize the listener.

Medicine Bear and Wawaskwane became very close that winter. They anxiously awaited their marriage at the first greening of spring. Wawaskwane, her mother, grandmother, and aunts had made new ceremonial clothing for the both of them. Medicine Bear, Meengun Kadeh, Zhingwak, and Small Fox had constructed a beautiful Odawa wedding lodge. Medicine Bear had shared much with the Cheyenne about the ways of his people, the Odawa Bear Clan. They were talking in the Odawa language as much as they did in Cheyenne. Medicine Bear was pleased that Wawaskwane would be comfortable in the customs and language when he took her back to his home. They had decided to make the long trip right after their marriage so that they would arrive before the next winter was upon them.

The warmth arrived just as abruptly as the cold had come many moons ago. The village was hastily preparing for the important event. Everyone had their own responsibilities so everything went smoothly and soon it was the day of the wedding. Because Medicine Bear had no family to rely upon, Wawaskwane's extended family took him under their wing. The feast food was readied; gifts were made for the couple to give to all in attendance, and the participants were arrayed in their ceremonial finest. Zhingwak began the procession to the flower bedecked valley by the river. His colorful seed-beaded buffalo robe and horned headdress attested his position as medicine man and spiritual leader of the village. Four pipe carriers, all in decorated buckskin, followed. Medicine Bear, Wawaskwane, her family, then the rest of the village came last.

The circle of life was made up of the people of the village. The pipe carriers stood in the four directions, East, South, West, and North, where they spread their bundles upon the ground in front of them. They began to prepare for the ceremony. A young man was chosen to carry the smoldering sage, sweet grass, cedar, and tobacco to smudge all of the people. He fanned the sacred smoke toward each person with a large eagle feather then placed the ashes into a brightly burning sacred fire, which was in the center of the circle. Zhingwak led Medicine Bear and Wawaskwane to the fire where they offered tobacco to the Great Spirit, the sky world, Mother Earth, and the four directions. Then they went back to Zhingwak where he began the sacred ceremony that joined a man and woman forever.

Zhingwak, in deference to Medicine Bear, said the sacred words not only in the Cheyenne language, but also in Odawa, just as he had said the passing on ceremony for Young Eagle. Medicine Bear was humbled by this gesture of consideration by the old medicine man. His heart was so full as he realized that he had finally found the love and respect that had eluded him all of his young life. He was so happy that he couldn't stop smiling. He looked at Flower and saw the same happiness mirrored in her face.

"I love you," he whispered to his wife. "I love you."

Medicine Bear and Wawaskwane spent their wedding night in the beautiful new lodge that had been a gift from Wawaskwane's father, grandfather, and brother. They slept until the sun was high in the sky, then they began to get ready for the long journey to the home of the Odawa. With all the feasts and celebrations, it took them the rest of the day to prepare to leave the next morning. Exhausted, they slept in their lodge the second night and awoke refreshed, ready to begin their new life together with an exciting adventure. They left early so as not to awaken anyone. All the farewells had been given the night before and Wawaskwane did not want to experience that sadness again. She didn't realize how hard it was going to be to leave the only home she had ever known and the only people she had ever loved. But the joy of being with the man she loved soon replaced her loneliness, and her excitement returned.

The brightly colored leaves were already falling by the time they had reached the place where the trails turned to the Northern direction. Medicine Bear couldn't travel as fast as he had with Young Eagle. Wawaskwane had to walk with her heavy burden, not run most of the way like the two young men did. It had already been five moons, Medicine Bear thought. He was worried about her. She was heavy with child and too tired to go very far at one time. He knew that they wouldn't make it home before the snow and cold winds came. Somehow he had to take care of his wife. He resolved to find a way to get them through this dilemma, even if he had to stop the journey right here and make a lodge to get them through the winter.

When Wawaskwane and Medicine Bear stopped for the day, they talked a long time about their situation. As they hungrily ate the smoked venison that they had prepared some time ago, they decided to find a suitable place to build their lodge. It took them a few more days but finally, on the banks of a swift river, they stopped and prepared to construct their winter home. Medicine Bear cut and smoothed the young maple, and Flower made strong rope from the basswood tree that had been soaking at the edge of the river. She gathered reeds and wove them into tight waterproof mats that would cover their dwelling, and also serve as a durable floor. The days flew by and the winds grew colder. Soon they were ready to begin.

Medicine Bear buried some of the poles deep into Mother Earth so that the winds would not blow the lodge down. He lashed these upright ones together tightly with the other poles that went around the framework, to form a large dome. When the smoke hole was finished, Flower handed him the mats to lash from bottom to top, overlapping slightly to keep out the rain and snow. Then he went inside, dug the fire pit in the center of the room, and placed large rocks around it to keep the fire contained. Flower had picked out her own cooking rock which was very flat and sat atop two of the others.

"I will cook you a delicious meal now, my husband," she said in her sing-song voice. "If you will catch a rabbit, I will see what Mother Earth has to offer us. We will have a feast to celebrate the first night in our new home."

Medicine Bear was so happy to see Wawaskwane in such good spirits that he rushed around laying the mats on the floor, brought in fresh cedar boughs for their bed, and placed the great bear skin on top of it. Then he gathered wood up into his huge arms and put it just inside of the door.

"Go gather then, my beautiful Flower, I will find you the biggest, most succulent wabose that you have ever seen!"

Medicine Bear was stretching the rabbit skin onto the drying rack when Wawaskwane returned. At the edge of the rapidly flowing river, she cleaned the fleshy roots that she had found on a grassy knoll. They went inside together and finished preparing the meal. Medicine Bear had already cut the rabbit into pieces, so Flower took down the iron pot that her mother had given her, and fried the meat to a golden brown. The pot had been made by the people that lived north of the big lakes. Her father had brought it back with him when he returned from a long trading trip. Medicine Bear had never seen a cooking pot before. He put more wood on the fire.

"So that is what made the load that I carried so heavy!" he growled in mock anger. "What else do you have hidden from me?"

They teased each other while Flower took water from the water basket and poured it into the pot to cover the meat and vegetables. They giggled like children as she cut up herbs with her sharp rock knife, then sprinkled them on top of the soup. Enticing smells were coming from the boiling pot, making Medicine Bear's stomach tighten. He ate with pleasure, thanking the Creator for this feast and for his beautiful Flower. Darkness closed in around the softly lit lodge. Soon

Medicine Bear and Wawaskwane were sound asleep, wrapped in each other's arms and in the fur of the giant bear.

Winter came with a vengeance. Drifts of snow nearly covered the lodge, but Medicine Bear and Flower stayed cozy and warm, and they had plenty to eat. They had worked hard to preserve enough food to last them the whole winter, and when they hungered for fresh meat, Medicine Bear would go and hunt. Flower was near delivery, so she spent her time making soft deerskin clothing for the new baby. Because she was so big, they talked of having more than one. Medicine Bear even made an extra large cradle board and lined it with lots of soft rabbit fur in case this was so.

One cold afternoon there was a scratching on the door flap. They had heard the snow crunching underfoot of what they had thought was a big animal. Medicine Bear took up a piece of firewood and went to see what four legged had dared to come to their lodge. Standing there was a woman. She seemed to be about the age of Flower's mother, but this was a stranger, a stranger that seemed slightly familiar to him. She greeted him in the Odawa way. Seeing that she was near frozen, he took her by the arm and led her to the fire. Flower was as surprised as Medicine Bear was. They didn't think that anyone but themselves were even close to this winter home that they had chosen. But they greeted her in the way of the Anishinabe, the way that their people had always welcomed a stranger. Flower gave her some hot soup and broke a large piece of quezhagun (bread) from the flat loaf, and gave it to her also. When she had finished her meal, the woman told them that her name was Neebin Qua.

"I have watched you from the woods ever since you came here," she said, looking toward Flower. "I have seen that your time is near so I came to help you with the birth. I have also been watching you, Medicine Bear. I have a story to tell you.

"When my husband and I were young, we had a male child.

In the beginning of his second year, we were traveling to visit my clan. We had come from the north, where the cold comes from. This is where my husband's clan was. He was Aleut, bear clan. His name was Bedoskah (when you first see the sun peeping out). Up river from here, there was a great storm. The river rose and washed away our shelter in the middle of the night. The waters were so angry that they wrenched my baby from my arms and took him with them. Bedoskah tried to follow the bobbing and weaving cradle board, but he was crushed by a huge tree that was ripped from Mother Earth by the winds and water. I became wedged between two trees with a third across my leg. I cried to the Great Spirit to let me live to find my baby. The waters washed the tree from my leg and I was free. Then I cared for my husband so that he could go west to Grandfather's lodge. His spirit stayed with me as I searched for my little son, and sustained me when I wanted to give up and follow him to the spirit world. I have spent all of my life searching this river and its banks for the child that I lost. Now, this day, my prayers have been answered."

Neebin Qua paused, happy tears rolling down her cheeks, and placed her hand upon Medicine Bear's cheek. "Medicine Bear, you look just like your father, Bedoskah. You are the little one that was taken from me. Now tell me your story."

Medicine Bear was astounded. He couldn't believe that this was his mother. He couldn't comprehend her story. All of his life he had thought that his mother had abandoned him because he was so ugly. Now he realized that this was not true. She did love him! He hugged her and they both wept, talking together all through the night. He told her of Nokomis finding him with the otters and even though she loved him, he always felt alone because of his looks. She told him of the many hardships that she had endured during her search. Finally, at the break of dawn, they slept.

In the early afternoon, Wawaskwane woke both of them.

Her waters had ruptured. Neebin Qua shooed Medicine Bear out of the lodge and began to prepare Wawaskwane, both physically and mentally, for her first birthing. Sometime in the night, Flower delivered a big baby boy. Neebin Qua bathed him and then placed him in his mother's arms. Both women said at the same time, "He looks just like Medicine Bear."

When Mother Earth turned green again, Medicine Bear, Wawaskwane, Neebin Qua, and Bedoskah started their journey to the home of the Odawa. Yes, Medicine Bear had named his son after his father, Bedoskah: when you first see the sun peeping out.